Title: Thoughts Without Borders Edged by Pen
Author: Tudor Moisa
Publisher: Independent Publishing Network
Publication Date: June 2023
ISBN: ISBN 978-1-80352-793-2

ISBN 978-1-80352-793-2

9 781803 527932 >

THOUGHTS
WITHOUT BORDERS
EDGED BY PEN

-TUDOR MOISA-

Table of Contents

PREFACE

***

TO THE READER

Three decades were a good lesson for me to observe the world and the people who live in it. One thing that defines me well is thinking about life and its circumstances, which are meant to be in our lives. I was going through so many, and life taught me so much; all these allowed me to see how complex life is, yet there is still so much to be discovered.

As the title says, *Thoughts without borders, edged by pen,* this expresses many thoughts I was dealing with within a couple of years; there were no borders, and they were coming into my mind one after another, yet I edged them by writing them down so others can understand life better. I do consider that every piece of art, when not revealed, is kept for the creator only. Once shared with others, art can be criticised from different perspectives. I chose to break these borders so others could avoid what I was struggling with, what I was going through. I have learned so much from those before me, and we are all meant to create a path for the next generation.

This book is formed from different quotes aiming to describe and highlight how we can create our lifestyle and reveal it constructively; however, this helps with understanding people, behaviours and actions by observing them closely. You don't need someone to express themselves by talking, but you can easily understand a lot if you know their lifestyle. Words and actions result from something that repeatedly happens until it becomes a lifestyle, defining you.

Applicability, perseverance, and experiences in doing something give so much value to what we are in the present and what we are about to become in the future. One of the quotes says: *The past is criticised by the present and still plans the future.* In other words, what we did in the past is nothing but what we are now, and it can plan the oncoming events, the future.

There is an excellent connection between actions and behaviour, and they impact one another; lifestyle is like a mirror; it reflects what's inside us; however, it can be seen as a strong imprint.

When it comes to success, every decision made in the past leads to what you are in the present; exercising prepares you for the future. Unfortunately, most are tempted to choose the quickest and easiest way without understanding that experiences are a good foundation for success. Listen to what others say but work hard to achieve your goals and let your actions speak more. In all you do, present your plans to the Almighty and await approval.

We can see something behind all these things in life, and this world stands on something. Life is the highest value we are offered, yet not everyone values life the most. The creation is nothing if there is no room for the Creator, and God can be found in nothing; when all these things disappear, there is room for God.

Another important chapter in life I highlighted in this book is family. If life is a one-time chess game, family represents the backline pieces that cannot be changed or turned into other pieces during the game. Challenges are on the other side of the table. After all, the beauty of winning the games is to defeat challenges with all your pieces on the table. The power stays in unity, not in a gathering.

As a thinker with a special dedication to wisdom, I understand where wisdom is rooted and the importance of guiding my life upon this. Through philosophy, we can study basic ideas about knowledge, truth, what is wrong or bad, religion, nature, and the meaning of life.

For a bit of amusement and laughter, humorous quotes imply the ability to perceive the comical and absurd in human life and to express these without bitterness. There is a need for humour to understand the meaning behind what is presented, and it is meant as a medium of education and not entertainment only.

In the end, I would like to encourage all seekers of wisdom to build up their lives rooted in truth and knowledge through education, good manners, and rules. Following this path, they will have healthy conduct. Some of the quotes may seem 'hard of digestion', but if people 'digest' them well, they can find the real meaning.

THE AUTHOR

London, 2023

Chapter 1: Lifestyle

19. The only way of observing the unstable is by standing on a solid rock of consciousness.

21. Knowledge – the finest weapon that can cause damage both ways.

27. Be prepared to make a stand, but don't stand unless it's really necessary!

29. The value of information is given by its applicability.

30. Same food on a different plate can be an insult.

31. The abnormality is accepted as normality due to the repetition of the abnormality until the normal becomes abnormal.

32. Knowledge means power, and yet I found so many weak.

33. Recharging your energy does not mean that you are wasting time; but instead you are preparing for an unexpectedly long journey.

35. The past is criticised by the present and still plans the future.

36. Elegant and classic are two values you will find on gentleman's territory.

63. If life is a game, any move you make will affect the player.

39. You can't become stronger unless you're exercising the weights.

41. Improving comes after challenge; if there is no challenge, there is no improvement.

45. Magic is an illusion, like many other things. Enjoy but don't let yourself be fooled by it easily.

47. Call yourself powerful if you can fill positions without changing the human state when transiting from one to another.

51. A strong or weak character is given by your position towards people.

52. Loyalty is a very rare precious value. When people find it by mistake, they don't know what it is, how to use it or where to put it. Most of the time it ends up in a forgotten old paper box.

55. When people talk, they cannot listen, and when they cannot listen, they cannot extend their knowledge.

56. People strive to rule over people, but they fail to rule over themselves.

57. People hear one side of the story, and they are tempted to judge as if they've seen and heard the entire one.

58. Hesitation can be considered a weakness unless it is planned.

60. In schools, we are instructed to interpret our experiences better. What if there are no experiences to interpret?

64. People have their own life stories. An attractive title does not mean great content.

65. Any kid wants to be grown, and any grown wants to be a kid again. We should live life and enjoy it at any stage in the present.

68. A lazy person is not stupid but cunning. Unconsciousness lies in the person who sustains the cunning with mercy.

72. When you ask for an explanation, be sure that you are ready to listen.

74. In reality, money does not buy your health, safety, rest, satiety, knowledge or happiness, yet you offer all that to get them. Set these dead figures to work for the living!

76. It's true that, as you walk up in life, the areas of knowledge get larger. Don't miss out that as you are reaching heights, the wind gets stronger.

77. Balance distance and time. Don't look too far, because you won't pay attention to what's happening underneath your nose. Don't go too slow, as you may not have time to reach your goals.

131. Toxic people will always hit you with their lousy content smell.

78. Two things you should not miss in life: being grateful for what you receive and dissatisfied with how much you give back.

79. The taste comes from the content. Don't be fooled by the packing. The majority ends up in the bin, after all.

81. When you think you are alone, don't stress too much, smile at yourself, it's much better than being sad in the crowd.

84. If an apple tree bears fruits and worms do not eat those fruits, either the apples are not healthy to be consumed, or they are protected by poison.

85. A fair trial does not refer to how many mistakes you make but to how ready you are to fix them.

89. A healthy seed touched by water sprouts; if this sprout has the right environment, it will grow and become a seed carrier. The comfort of having the grains sitting in a dry bag does not help, as they will get eaten after all.

90. When a ton of gold sits on a detonator, don't be greedy for the gold; defuse the explosive first. It is better to last a lifetime than to lose a life to have it.

94. Disappointment is the degraded nature, well dressed in pride, that can do nothing but smile at you after the damage is done.

95. In the past, men worked hard to look as ferocious as possible; today, they are paying to look as soft as possible. Be like the old-school guys, fearless.

96. If our body is 75% water, we need to work for the rest of 25% to become shapeless and formless.

97. Patriotism is one of the old powerful weapons used to create wars between civilians. We have a planet, not a country, we must care for.

99. Tell no one who your enemies are. Even your friend would use them when you made a mistake towards him.

100. I like water because it cools down the heated discussions started from a thirst for quarrels.

105. If someone screams, it doesn't mean they don't want to listen to you; your presence only strikes their ears. Likewise, the wind has no sound; only the things that stay in the way make noise.

109. Bowing your head is a gesture of nobility, not inferiority. The ability to stand is when you know the lowlands better than the peaks.

111. Sated people will not be full forever; they must be mindful that hunger returns fast without GPS and asks for more.

112. Your knowledge and intelligence should not put the listener on the bench, but it should help the listener to engage for improvement. If the listener does not engage, you have learned nothing.

113. If you are at the table and someone else chooses your food, you are either a child or a person with disabilities.

116. A great cook is not the one who lives to cook but the one who makes you wish to stay alive.

119. Sometimes, to say nothing can be the most thoughtful quote that others can never reproduce.

121. While some struggle to discover others' stories, others work to make their own story as engaging as possible.

123. If you have enriched your education with the help of the uneducated and you have not shared its discovery, you are a killer of freedom.

124. If anyone tells others your secrets, they were no secrets in the first place.

130. Life can be considered a dance. Sometimes, stepping back and forward seems to look like you do not have a specific direction, but it can be judged as modern if you keep the rhythm.

133. Even when the traitor is loyal, they can never be trusted.

134. It is very easy to forget the person who sowed once someone else has picked the harvest.

135. Stay away from people known for their ability to bring out the worst in other people so that they can have a reason for their dark actions.

140. The more you try to hide, the more visible you become.

141. When you ask anyone, you will receive any answer. If you are looking for a specific answer, try to find a specific person to ask.

143. There are two types of villains in this world: those who are busy with their own dream and those who do not have a dream but talk about the dream of others like they have a personal one.

144. Never awake the fury of a patient man.

145. When you are in a hole, dig, you might get to see the other side of the story.

146. We can never see perfection through flawed thinking. Can the rain be imperfect?

147. The bigger you get, those closer become unnoticed and die due to the shadow created by your size. So always make a correct mobile distance if you want to stay alive in the game.

148. Be so well known that to be understood will no longer be needed.

154. We cannot change the past, but we can always take notes and change the future.

158. Different perspective always helps excellent judgment.

160. The tree can grow even when a branch is dead, as long as the roots are healthy.

163. Books explain you the knowledge; experience gives you understanding.

164. When a snake pulls back, be careful, the following action is deadliest.

166. When you're silent, you practice listening; when you're listening, you improve your knowledge. When you know, you start planning, and when you're planning, you have the chance to succeed. When you grow, they should listen to your silence.

167. Talk wisely when at least expected, draw attention, and then let them starve for more.

170. An early judgment on a sheep can make you feel its cold bite, and then it's too late to call it a wolf. Be careful with the old sheep!

173. Any blast without prediction is the most effective and harmful explosion.

174. If I take you up on my shoulders, don't assume that I will let you control my legs.

176. Never serve good food in a dirty dish if you want the food to be eaten clean. Instead, clean the plate before putting food in it to eat it with an appetite.

178. Don't change your food all at once, even if the offer seems exciting. Change it gradually so you won't get intoxicated and die.

179. The biggest mistake young people make is to think that they know enough when enough is the invisible prison that keeps their ears closed when the elders preach knowledge.

181. If you kill the elderly, the only thing left will be theories.

182. What's the point of having wings if you're working to build your own cage?

184. If you are in the sea and the waves beat and make your swimming difficult, do not start fishing.

185. Don't waste time talking about yourself, instead, work on a character to be like honey on the lips of others.

186. The perfect meal is the one that keeps you alive.

189. If the information is not tested, no value can be given. What you think is a diamond may turn out to be something else that cannot pass the test when placed on a diamond press.

195. Flatteries are like roses; pleasant to look at and sharp to pick.

196. Destroy your best friend, and you will create your worst enemy.

210. When a leopard attacks a bark, every step made is precise and soundless, followed by a long wait until it reaches the prey. When you think it is close enough to

the prey to attack without problems, the cat waits. She does not lose her energy by making her presence heard or making unnecessary moves to attract someone's attention. The feline is waiting for a single sudden move, and this should be decisive. Remember: people who look gentle and don't seem to do the right thing when you think they should, you might be amazed to see that they suddenly turn out to be the most accurate predator.

217. Extinguish the spark until it is called fire. A catastrophe can be stopped with a contra catastrophe that creates another catastrophe.

218. The rest of the time is the most valuable; considering that most of the time is spent on the rest, that is invaluable.

220. A good thought said by a madman is like a flower that smells good and grows on a pile of manure.

222. Pay attention to the ones that do not respect the household servants while sitting at your table. It's an insult brought to you from a sitting edge as they are not big enough to stand you on the field.

224. A dog shouldn't bark to be fierce but should know when to bite to be left alone.

226. A knife, no matter how sharp, does not cut if there is no resistance.

228. The taste of a food cannot be decided by the looks of the dish or by a single try. The more you try, the more you discover.

229. If the mouth represented us in the performance of use, we would all get first place with a medal; if the ear represented us, we would often be unable to fit even the last place. Try to hear the silence talking.

230. Build yourself behind a curtain, even if that curtain is the old you.

232. If you want to see someone inside without too much fuss, open their fridge.

234. Whoever does not respect your intimacy indirectly doesn't respect your intimacy directly, either.

244. If the discussions are just interpretations of thoughts, it means that the thoughts can be good but can be misinterpreted by the sound of the voice.

245. If you see a sharp chisel, you see a chisel that cuts air, the chisel that creates diamonds is blunt.

247. So much preparation to share a topic and so little preparation to listen to the topic when presented.

248. If a youth says that he has nothing to lose because he is too young to be judged harshly by the elders, it is wrong. I would say that if you lose your start, the remedy can be very expensive.

250. If your mouth cannot stay shut, what do you expect from others?

254. I don't occupy my beautiful moments taking pictures. The beautiful moments are to be lived not to be immortalised.

256. When people say: 'I've heard good or bad things about you', I answer them: 'Are you sure this is not the only thing you have sought to hear?'

259. When you don't have the experience of a farmer, you usually consider daisies the perfect food for pigs. That's why some daisies are different in price.

260. A fair fight for equality is when you are on the advantageous side, not on the disadvantaged side, willing to pull the progress down for you to reach.

261. Never look the past in the eyes; it's not developed as the present and can be a disable for the future.

262. When I see children talking about life, I tell them: 'Be careful not to get tripped on your sleeves.'

264. When you are born, you know all the good. As you grow older, you begin to learn what others know.

268. People are afraid to discover the truth; they don't understand that the undiscovered truth is, in fact, the most toxic lie.

275. The benefits are an insult to my intelligence.

276. If you want to hear the water whistle, bring it to a boil with a hand over its mouth.

277. The taste of hunger creates master chefs even when they serve food for pigs.

278. When you pass through the valley of weeping, you can collect the most precious crystals.

281. Once you tell your friends your position, the enemies will prepare.

284. A good dog, accepted in a yard, marks its ground as a rule of dominance and protection. If you ever decide to leave the dog behind, hungry, the dog's first instinct will be to go back to its marked place, not to its owner.

251. Beware of gossipy people. When they've finished talking about others, they start talking about you. Gossip is not information but misinformation. Gossip can be compared with a flower, a moulded flower and eventually, you are going to get sick.

288. If you are on-trend with being open-minded, perhaps you should consider having an updated antivirus.

291. Answering questions means stopping to think.

294. Never start a fight if you feel the smell of a coward in your team. Eliminate the bad smell first; a coward friend is the worst enemy.

297. People say that I'm too silent. Maybe they're too deaf to hear what I'm saying.

298. I'm telling you ten-year-old stories so I can write another one quietly now.

300. Every small scar can be a big story to tell.

301. People are fair until they have to tell the truth.

309. Never judge the competency of a builder by the way he talks. He can be mute and a great craftsman. If you go after the one who only speaks, you will be left with a nice story, sleeping under the wide sky.

310. The more you dig for something, the more valuable the find becomes. Having your values in the hands of anyone will make them worthless, and they will easily be mistreated.

313. When you make a mistake, stop, and don't reverse. To reverse means to move forward in another direction.

324. He who knows the truth will be taught he was a slave of the information before him.

325. The rules must be obeyed as their master, not as an enslaved person, otherwise, you will live locked in a cage even if you are free.

330. Education is for those who seek no comfort in riches but makes the riches to comfort the poor.

332. Naturalness is the most expensive card to play, and yet so many use it as a base coat.

333. The one thing that is imperative to achieve a dream is to have a good sleep.

334. Resources create opportunities, opportunities create desires, and desires combined with facts create successes. Removing any step from the process will change the result.

339. Never praise the prey in front of people. The hungrier they get, the more stupid they become. Instead, eat, get ready and show strength in battle.

341. Whoever fights calmly has a better chance of hitting the target.

342. Never be distracted by the one who speaks loudly. Seek the one who listens in shadows; he is the one who can make moves hard to be discovered.

343. Being safe from what is safe and natural means being unsafe and ill.

345. Lies in words can hide the truth in deeds. Truth in words can never hide a lie in deeds.

349. I would not bow before the poor to show them that I have nice shoes; instead, I would stand as poor in front of the rich to show them that I can still grow up to see the sky with my head held high.

356. The madman ends up taking his own life with his own brain.

357. If you throw garbage at a plant, it will grow healthier and more beautiful.

359. If someone saves you from drowning by throwing a torn plank from their boat, show respect to him, even if you become a captain of an imperial ship.

360. From a distance, people perceive you as a giant or a louse. Get closer, for the correct examination.

363. Many times I thought that if you think many times, you use your own brain, not others.

364. If you want to be heard by the crowd that follow your enemy, mention his name and half of the battle is won.

376. When a friend that became an enemy needs you, allow him to become a memory.

377. If you only have a mouth to speak, you definitely do not have ears to listen to.

379. For the water to hit the shore, it must empty from the other side.

384. Wise is the one who asks the question, smart is the one who answers, and stupid is the one who doesn't ask, thinking he knows everything. What would you know now if you hadn't asked? You would have known what others would have placed in front of you. Be a wise man and ask the right question.

385. When you give an intelligence award to a madman, it's like saying that the pig is a good example of a clean pharmacy.

201. We are quick to be judged with judgment for kids when it comes to making mistakes as adults, but we never accept to listen like kids when we are put on a bench by the innocence of a child.

205. For some people, a hug can mean life and be treated as a souvenir when received. It doesn't cost you anything to be nice.

386. The food you cook should not have smell but taste. If the food is cooked and has a pleasant smell, it will attract the starved of all categories, especially the greedy ones. If the food cooked has no smell but a good taste instead, you will be able to choose who you want to feed; that way you will not be killed for your good deed.

389. Weeds and corn grow in the same garden, and yet one is digestible and the other is not. The habit of weeds is to appear first in the light and choke out the corn. If that garden has a gardener, the corn will survive, and the weeds will be cut before they become too strong to kill. Don't be too quick to judge a garden by how green it is; clean it, and you won't starve.

390. The wise jump from the midst of nonsense like corn from hot oil.

395. When there is a drought, the weeds dry quickly; only the trees with strong roots resist. Concentrate on growing good roots during good weather, the branches will grow naturally.

400. Sometimes, you need to eat garbage so that you come to appreciate a portion of good food.

402. Media shows the reality until you hit the screen when trying to follow it blindly.

406. A human being falls quicker if he's hit from the inside rather than the outside.

407. There will be a time when you must pick up the sword and fight, even if that is just the word. Don't just wait; prepare yourself, and when the time comes, let them all watch the real killer blow.

408. My life is too interesting to start talking about others' affairs.

409. The reason that a predator does not kill more than he can eat is that he likes its food fresh.

411. People locked in their brains have also lost the key. The key to unlocking it and becoming open-minded is knowledge.

412. Until the dust is settled on the ledge, don't open your eyes or walk; be patient and wait until the next step is clear to make.

413. While walking past a ruin, I noticed that there was no one there now to talk about the beauty of the place or what remained from what it used to be when this was a building, even out of envy. Now few try to understand what shape the ruin had as a building; sometimes, it is discovered or covered by the wind, and it is fascinating. A ruin is not to be conquered but a building in all its splendour. I can compare this with us as beings. If your body is hit physically or mentally, it means that you are not a ruin, but there are still values that some want to destroy or take from you to build theirs. Don't fall into depression; instead, be strong and rebuild what was damaged, find ways to defend it better, and keep your conscience awake. There are so many out there; some are undercover enemies.

415. A strong mind will punish the body itself for wrongdoing. The weaker the body, the harder the punishment.

420. You can find wealth hidden in health by living a clean life and poverty behind the dresser.

425. If you throw a stone into the wind, it will fall like a rock. You might change their shape if you throw a stone between the stones. Change comes in a collision.

426. Mastering poison makes you the holder of the true hidden secrets.

428. Do not go to the man who sticks branches in the ground and says: 'I have planted forests', go to the man who sows, even if, at first, nothing is visible.

429. Weeds prefer tilled soil.

433. A battle is better handled from a sitting position.

437. You know that a fruit is ripe not by its colour but by the sound made when you crush it.

438. What do you think about this: A lion cub's roar sounds more like a cat's meow when angry, creating a disadvantage for its position in battle. As soon as it grows, the lion finds that the anger can be concentrated to the advantage of its strength and ferocity. Never underestimate an animal by its sound. A lion cub may sound like a cat but is still a formidable predator.

455. The more united we are, the closer we are to being human.

457. Men, as much as they would like to, cannot keep anything forever.

463. Good food is the one that loves you from the inside.

468. Never draw water from a well with a stick. You won't have a chance to quench your thirst and the water will become cloudy.

470. Regardless of how well it is made or how good the food is, if it has a drop of poison, even the dish must be thrown away.

471. Any good soldier will know that the uniform is there to hide him from the enemy. Suitable clothing is for the right occasion.

Chapter 2: Success

1. Successful people are not represented by how they look but by how they think.

2. One step up the valley is the step to reach the heights.

10. Don't get upset when they talk about you; that makes them interesting!

12. Every decision made in the past leads to the person you are in the present. Exercise your brain now so you can be prepared for the future!

17. People look at me like I'm crazy when I present new ideas, but when they work, people call me a genius.

18. Most are tempted to choose the quickest way, thinking this is the way to success, while others think there is no way to succeed and leave their life to pass by. Few people are on the right path but are too obstructed to see it.

22. True leaders are ready to serve first and be served last.

23. The difference between the predator and the prey is that one is after resources and the other is the resource.

28. Behind any success, there is a hassle.

34. Listen to what others might have to say; it might be the right solution for you!

38. Everyone wants to succeed, but few are ready to face the challenge.

40. No one speaks or does things behind you unless you are ahead of them.

44. 'Rich' does not mean having money but the ability to create lasting values.

46. I use my numbers to invest in people; others use their people to invest in numbers. Who do you think is winning?

48. The beauty of being a coach is when the teacher listens to the lesson taught by his student and takes notes.

53. The unexpected should be considered the most expected when creating a strategy of any type.

61. The source of imagination leads entrepreneurs to nail their talents.

66. I prefer to be exhausted, not poor and comfortable.

70. If you are not losing focus in the process, you will be able to embrace the result with a smile on your face.

75. A virus that's weakening and can destroy people's morals is the fear of others' judgment.

80. Train for valleys while you are up on the mountain. If you do so, the problems appearing in valleys will be solved out of habit.

83. Water can caress or cut; it all depends on speed. Control the speed, and you will have the result that you are looking for.

87. A precious stone brought from the bottom floor of the ocean by waves must be picked by an artist and placed on a beautiful necklace that can be worn on special occasions. All those events must line up perfectly; otherwise, that precious stone can be just a forgotten stone on the bottom floor of the ocean.

92. Learn to manage with little or no money. When you succeed, you will be able to manage values.

93. If you want to win, don't start the game until you have all the pieces arranged on the table.

103. Real success is not when people follow or like your work but when they copy and practice what they see you doing.

104. If you have questions, don't wait for someone to hand you the answer. Instead, get to work, find them yourself and deliver the result to help the world's progress.

106. Don't get upset by someone who tells you to take off the coat of laziness and put on the coat of diligence. Instead, be upset about the coat of laziness that keeps you heavy.

107. A successful person will never talk about his successes but about his failures. Managing failure after failure without losing the passion for trying makes you strong and will create a successful person.

108. Success doesn't need publicity. If the world doesn't see it, you're still in process.

110. Limits are there for people that don't know there is no limit; there is just education to handle freedom.

114. Build a round table for no one inside to feel the need to plot around corners and build a strong group for no one outside to understand who is orchestrating.

118. It doesn't matter how small the weapon is as long as the blast created can mark history.

125. Never judge someone by his appearance but by his deeds.

126. Any rat that comes to light should pay attention to hawks.

127. People who dare to go through failures will have a chance to succeed, but people who claim to have gone through failures will not know what success means and will get stuck in the process.

129. Mixing people is essential. Having a cocktail is much stronger than having a drink made from a single fruit.

132. The best hack to get rich is to know when to play poor.

136. It doesn't matter how big the gun you have as long as the one with no gun controls you.

137. Imagining others as you want them to be will not reach your expectations in any way; some are just well-dressed and mediocre.

142. Your criticism helps the success of others. No one wins but the players who take criticism to better themselves.

149. I might be tired sometimes, but I still have my eyes open for any opportunity.

155. Walk and talk; the most productive when you don't have time to sit.

156. Even when the base seems to be impregnable, success says perseverance.

169. Collect more water from a slight tap with a good bucket than from a waterfall with a broken bucket.

223. It's not about who scored numerous goals, it's about who scored the most spectacular one.

227. There is no satiety in business. The more you do, the hungrier you are.

233. No one should be interested in how you fall but in how fabulous you get up.

316. The need accepts any payment.

320. If you are good enough, you will become the perfect shark catch.

172. Cleverness is not measured by how old you are but by how you act, often unmasked by the so-called inexperienced.

180. Don't call yourself strong when everyone supports you, but rather call yourself strong when everyone is against you, and you're still standing.

183. Any sniper should know that impatience can endanger the target.

187. I have realised that if you mention no money, people who are a cost will disappear eventually.

188. Have no expectations from people, and you will be delighted to see them bringing even small results.

192. Would you believe someone who says the same thing you say, knowing how the person thinks? If you don't believe that person, don't expect someone to believe you when you say, 'Trust me'.

193. If you're not an asset to the company you work for, all actions made by you using the platform will

weaken the business, and in reality, the company becomes a working asset for you.

194. Don't call anyone a loser if they still have a chance to win.

197. Whoever has never endured having a boss, does not know how to treat an employee.

204. When a leader is mindless, people suffer; and when the people start to weep, the presence of a wise leader is necessary.

206. When you go to give a speech, take not only the words with you but the wisdom as well.

211. You can always buy a title no matter how expensive it is, but you can never buy the experience, no matter how much money you have.

219. If you are not able to lose or ever lost something, do not try to give advice on how to recover to the ones that have lost already.

236. A lion walks tactilely, not because he is not afraid of hyenas but because he wants his attention not to be disturbed by his own noise.

237. A louse that dies on a cow's tail and one that dies on a king's head. The place where you expose your talent counts more than the talent itself.

238. You don't have to talk to be heard by people, especially if you displease them with success.

242. The more you ride your bike, the more confident you will get into dangerous corners at speed without touching their sides.

243. Money is the chain of the brain. You still work for welfare, but now it's voluntary, not tied in visible chains.

273. People are made for success regardless of position as long as they do it well; for example, it can also be a landfill worker position.

274. Success does not mean clean or dirty but using each person's skills responsibly.

283. Money that does not bring happiness is pocket change.

285. If someone tells you in minutes that they can make you £1 billion in a year, tell them they owe you £1 thousand for the minutes spent in the conversation. If they don't pay it, stop listening to them. Nobody helps you without interest.

290. Some people prefer to buy bigger slippers, thinking they will live to grow their feet, not understanding that big slippers slow them from running towards success.

296. The poor create prey from everything instead of creating the potential for anything. That's why the poor will become poorer, and the rich will become even richer.

302. If I choose to sit at the table of those who party, I am judged for wasting my time; if I choose not to sit there, I'm judged for ignorance. The incapacity is not for those trying to develop knowledge but for those who will not increase the circle.

303. Fake is one of today's true deals. If you can trade fake as currency between counterfeits, you can call yourself successful.

304. If you want to kill a dream, shoot him in the head.

308. Managing people and managing numbers is not one and the same thing. Numbers will not argue, try people.

311. The weak point of anything is the one through which it can be manipulated.

314. When you suddenly reach the top without knowing the process, you will be kicked down to learn the process the other way around.

323. To be rich means to have the ability to dream. Dreams are the blueprints of tangible things.

328. When people call me lucky, I say my one is called perseverance.

347. A good leader is a good follower. In our world, the chance for a follower to become a true leader is almost zero to impossible. If a leader tells you he will make you a leader, be prepared to be his number one follower. A true leader will always encourage loyal followers to pass on his word. The question is: If a leader creates leaders that create leaders, who are going to follow? And if there are no followers, who are to be called leaders? The ways of becoming a leader are to accept the follower's position or to implement your own rules for someone to follow.

351. If you follow the rules, you might have a chance to get to the top to change them. If you get to the top, you will no longer change the rules as they are no longer for you to follow.

355. Don't expect to be understood by people who think differently if you think differently.

362. Experience comes with exercising mistakes.

365. The mouth is the gate to your thoughts. Making no sound will keep your plans safe.

372. Even when you have failure after failure, persevering in failure will make you successful.

374. Some people are saying: 'I need more work to have more money'; I would encourage them to look for a better-paid job so they can spend time thinking about how to get a better-paid job.

375. There is no free time. There is used time or wasted time.

378. To beat a problem, you have to take the shape of the problem.

391. The most hidden enemy comes up to you in the daytime.

393. The worst enemy of your body is indiscipline.

396. Never trust someone more than your gut. In the end, it's your gut that will pay the price anyway.

397. When two cows are drowning, save the milky one, not the fat one.

398. The collapse of the hill is the fear of the valley being covered by heavy rocks, and the valley is the fear of the hill being swallowed up regardless of the height. Never think you are too high to be reached or too low to fall.

399. Animals that make sounds are easily discovered and usually become prey instead of predator, but any animal that moves in silence is deadly.

401. Hiring someone to carry your burdens means wishing that you would atrophy.

410. The volume of work dictates the price.

414. Don't prepare your enemies with tells about your successes; surprise them.

417. The answer to a good living is not to fight for a better-paid job but for an existence free of charge.

421. In general, people who sit next to you are those people who don't know how you do things. Once they find out the secret, they go and do it themselves.

430. It does not take a dog to bark the character of a lion. A lion is a lion by construction.

434. A tree that gives good fruits is never advertised in the market.

435. Don't wait for time to pass. Time will pass without you caring. Work as much as you can, and if you do so, you will end up having something more than the time waited for.

440. If you want to become rich, don't work for the poor.

436. Finding a problem is very important. There is no solution without finding the problem. So, when someone asks what the problem is, they actually don't want to work to find the problem.

439. It's useless to have a big pot if it's broken, and it's useless to have it beautiful if you can't use it. Better to enjoy a small and good bowl in which you can gather, even if it fills up quickly.

448. The one who sounds the horn is the most vulnerable on the battlefield. He announces that the enemy can expose his position and strategy.

451. If you don't know the real in detail, you will be fooled by any fake.

454. When you laugh about the person who falls, you did not reach any of their heights before. Only people who are down are laughing about the ones who fall, as they are the only ones who can see it happening.

452. If you stay close to the waters, eventually, you will get wet.

453. A poor man in things weeps the wealth of the poor in the mind who laughs in the face of poverty.

458. Never strike a deal after a glass of wine.

461. Potential defines beauty.

462. There is a need for dirty hands to show the way to clean success.

464. I could pay a lot of people to talk about me, but no one would do it better than my deeds.

465. Be a man who makes a lot of noise when he's silent.

466. If I ended up creating a name out of good words, someone always needed to shout them for the name to be heard. If I create a name out of good deeds, I won everyone's ear even when silent.

473. Trying is the duty of every man.

Chapter 3: Spirituality

4. Present your plans to the Almighty and then await for approval.

20. Life is the highest value people can have, yet not everyone values life the most.

25. Make your pilgrimage to be the most wanted reading book!

42. No matter how great the creation can be, the creation may be useless if there is no room for the Creator to present its functionality.

50. No one is free; nothing is ours. We know so little, and yet we are so good at acting when it comes to it.

54. As scary as darkness can look, it can be as helpless in the face of light.

59. One of the best books to read is the universe itself.

62. Knowledge does not have a beautiful shape, and still, it is beautiful; it does not have strength, and still, it is powerful.

69. We will grow 'till this planet finds no place for us, and then we will change dimensions.

73. When you hear me talking to myself, never interrupt! I am consulting a real friend.

82. If your body fails to listen, your conscience suffers. If your conscience gives up the council, everything you think you have will crumble. Don't neglect your conscience!

86. While you walk through the dark, don't forget that you can always use the light given. Sometimes having the light, but not using it doesn't really help.

88. To be wise, you don't need to wait a lifetime to get it, but the desire to prostrate yourself before the eternal wisdom, ask for it, and be ready to receive it.

91. If we are in deep water for a long time, all we want to see is a piece of land; if we are in the desert for a long time, all we want to see is water; if it's too hot, we want ice, and if it's cold, we want warm. We are so strong when we measure the muscles between us, but we are so soft and weak when we face nature.

115. A beautiful thing sent out of hatred is like the rose that scratches you when you hurry to catch a train.

122. We are so distracted by art and neglect the artist who can create more art for our entertainment.

128. The universe is like a mechanism that works perfectly. Therefore, if we look for world order, we should reinstate it, not implement a new one.

138. Forgiving and acting like you know nothing are two rules for keeping peace in place.

150. The most challenging moment for a doctor is to be helpless in the face of death after helping many to face it successfully.

151. When you're young, you believe you have all power and knowledge to overcome any challenge; the older you get, the more you realise how unknowledgeable and vulnerable you are.

153. With how many masks people have now, Halloween does not celebrate masking but exposes the dark parts of a person.

157. When you say "Nature", you say "Extraordinary"!

159. Your style is your eternal trademark.

161. Man's words can defect nature's image.

162. Even when small, any flicker of light in darkness will draw attention.

165. Death is a supreme verdict that the creator can only give. Some try to steal it; few find it by mistake; only the courageous ones are waiting for it.

168. Not every big gets noticed, and not every small pass is unnoticeable.

175. Education without morality creates monsters.

191. People do not understand that the power does not remain in what is shown, but in what is hidden and continues to create movement.

199. To the rich of today, the deeds are no longer seen after they are made but before.

212. We ended up posing with the dead to show we were still alive.

213. Humans have infinity in their heads, which is why they can't stop progress, regardless of whether this progress is called life.

231. When you want to see living art, go to nature!

239. Sin does not allow you to think divinely.

249. In reality, people create copies of art. If you want to see the original art, look at the nature that is renewed from year to year.

252. Human beings don't know how to manage the good; that's why they end up doing the bad.

253. To notice the intelligence of a creator, try to break down his creation into individual parts and then try to put them back.

257. Some fool themselves into saying that they have their own way of life. I would say that the road and the signs are already there by the creator. What you can own are your actions to the signs.

202. If you want to go to heaven, you have to get rid of the riches of the world's teachings and get poor from everything that is called earthly.

269. As long as I live here on earth, I will train my silence to be heard loud after I leave.

270. The sound of clean deeds has a much more tempting smell than the sound of an airy mouth.

305. God can be found in nothing. When all things disappear, there is room for God.

307. The human body is the gate through which the soul can experience life on Earth. Without it, contact with the planet is invisible. Try everything without affecting anybody or any soul, and then share the result with humanity to be a lesson for the ignorant.

315. The eyes of the world will blind your eyes to seeing reality.

317. Hiding a code in art is divine.

319. If you understand God, he is either not God, or you are not human.

322. Nature can be read, but this is not for the illiterate.

326. When people come to understand how beautiful life is, they will realise that they have been kept dead by needs that do not exist.

331. The human mind is so complex that trying to understand it would be like trying to pave a road on the Milky Way to the universe.

336. If you turn off the light, the darkness can see all your sides.

346. There is no ugly in nature; there is clean or unclean. All creation is good.

348. Never sell something immortal for something that is mortal or dead.

353. Pretending to be rich in front of people will make you poor in front of life.

354. If everything was made out of nothing, then nothing is GOD.

361. In a desert, if you find a blade of grass, you are as excited as if discovering the secret of life.

368. If there are people out there with souls and people without souls, who guides the ones without?

369. The only thing that you need to do in life is to live it. Don't try to live someone else's life or leave someone else to live your own, as this is a failure in itself.

371. If life can be described as a colour, painting a masterpiece will require it to be colourful.

380. If all that surrounds us is evolution, then the assumption of things should not exist.

382. A living being is an active link between the soul and the earth. When the soul is called back to its master, the earth returns from whence it was taken. Invest wisely, your soul can be called next.

388. In the cemetery, no one is jostling for position, everyone is waiting for the order in silence.

392. The pain leaves your body as soon as it finishes killing the weak in you.

394. Invest in real estate and the government can take that; invest in people and that can be taken by death; invest in the art of surviving and the only one who can take that is God.

403. Something that was given as the first gift from God to man when man was found unhappy is now dressed and presented for others to look at and desire. Men are becoming increasingly a good platform to present their own gifts for others to use.

404. Acting rich or poor is in the hands of the actor himself. What film is he playing in? Depends on the script. If you want to change a line in the film, talk to the Producer.

405. If you place your life in the hands of humans, you will find yourself enslaved by their ambition. If you place your life in the hands of the Creator, He will give you freedom.

419. A man who is dead to himself can no longer be killed by anyone.

422. The most skilled at life are those who die.

423. Find a vulnerability in anything, call it sin and then create the law.

424. A good man is a man who keeps evil in check.

427. Eyes closed to the world are eyes open to the soul.

431. Good people die first. They have demonstrated their ability to move to the next level.

432. When the soul leaves the body, whatever remains on this earth smiles with the hands across the chest.

441. If Adam was brought to life with God's breath in his nostrils, then one of the ways of keeping God's breath on earth is through human reproduction.

443. The word of God is not interpretable, but people's understanding of it can vary. For example, sighted people can see colours and agree upon the colour that matches the description, but blind people can describe what they think about what they feel a thing looks like. The colours remain the same for both; however, their understanding and explanation can vary.

444. Whoever wants to work with me must have God's vision; whoever wants my place must have God's permission, and whoever wants to be like me must break God's decision.

449. The difference between dream and vision is that at one, you have to enjoy sleep, and at the other, you must be awake.

450. In the cemetery, there are no contradictions, everyone smiles silently.

459. Poor people collect gold and money all their lives and then die with only a dream of riches. Great people gather dying dreamers and awake them for eternity.

460. God made me a favour by letting me use my money intelligently to get almost broken. I understand now that without Him I am a wealthy poor man.

Chapter 4: Family

3. Take care of others as you take care of yourself.

6. Count on someone who has your back for no reason.

8. My son, give yourself no rest in doing good, thinking of how short this life can be! Make the best out of it!

11. If life is a one-time chess game, the family are the backline pieces that cannot be changed or turned into other pieces during the game; friends are the second line of pieces that can be changed or turned into pieces that favour the position of the backline, and on the other side of the table are the challenges. The beauty of winning the game is defeating challenges with all your pieces on the table.

16. People king's words are given to the son of the right hand, who shouts them from the wolf counsel's rooftop, and the world receives them as a gift.

37. Photos can be a reminder of places, people, and moments. Try to be where memories of people and moments will not displease you!

43. Many of them gather, but very few of them understand the power of unity.

67. There must be a hive and honeybees that are working collectively to create honey. Any bee that tries to live outside the colony dies famished.

101. Flying alone in a circle can strengthen your wings, but the world will feel sorry for you. However, flying together in a circle will make the world wonder and cheer you for the circus created.

139. An ideal conquest is made only in unity. So, if people want to conquer freedom, first, they need to understand what freedom means, and then they must kill the ego that pulls them apart.

216. When a dog stops the wolf's howl and thinks it's great, that's why he's not attacked; he should run away to save his life until others come. It is known that wolves attack in packs.

240. A tsunami does not start from the edges to attack a point, but it starts from a point, and the farther it goes, the bigger and stronger it becomes. Never attack the family that gave you birth.

241. The mountains rise or fall depending on what pushes them to rise and what pulls them apart to fall. Be one of the ones pushing the circle you are part of if you want to be seen as part of an extraordinary mountain.

255. My expression sometimes has the features of a royal chariot wheel due to the fact that I wandered a lot on the roads of the commune. I support and give mobility to the royalty by rolling in the dust and mud.

266. Above a king is a mother and a father without whom his existence would not be human.

295. If you want to sit at my table, build your chair; otherwise, you will be treated as a servant.

299. People are like letters: if you use BDT as a configuration, it will mean "Bangladesh taka"; if you use TBD, it can be understood as "to be discussed". The same letters arranged as BTD will mean "brothers till death". By changing your position, you will change the entire meaning for everyone.

321. Girls who dream of rich partners must get ready to give their baby boys rich growth. Girls who dream of strong partners must get ready to give their baby boys challenging growth. If your generation does not do that for the generation to come, all you do is repeat the same mistake that your mother made.

338. Man's definition is given by the woman who helps him, when present, to discover his nature.

350. If you lose your family, you lose your bloodline; if you lose your bloodline, you lose your life. If you lose your life, you are a dead man walking.

358. Even the trees, if they come from the same root, beat each other when the wind blows.

367. When you are a kid, you are in a cage; when you get married, you get back into the cage.

445. If you want to be a queen for your man, treat him like a king; if you want to be a dishonoured woman by your man, treat him like a dishonourable man. How you treat your man defines your status.

446. Not strong branches or green leaves define a good tree, but it's fruits that bring satiety and health to your body.

447. Until a mason sets his hand to build, bricks are just forms of clay.

456. Don't marry the woman that has the nicest appearance, marry a woman who is healthy and has wisdom. Healthy to produce strong children and wisdom to raise them for life.

469. Until I realized that work educates my ability to understand home life, and home life helps my behavioural work ethic, I thought that these two things needed balancing. These are necessary for communion so that you grow as a person in society.

Chapter 5:
Philosophy/Others

7. Simple is the complexity of things, actions, or feelings that make sense.

9. Stand on solid soil and look through clear gas to see the beauty of the liquid reflection.

14. Sometimes, taking the sunglasses off makes you see the world brighter.

15. Taking a slice out of a cake does not make the slice bigger but the cake smaller.

24. The tree that lives in a dry environment has its roots growing deep in the ground. When the storm comes, the tree stands like it has been hit by a breeze, and if cut off, it will grow back stronger.

26. The fear of loss does not disappear until it is confronted.

49. The mirror reflects everything in front of it, and yet it is one of the most reliable that can hold up secrets.

71. If I'm silent, that doesn't mean I don't know the answer, but sometimes the loudest sound may have no reception.

98. Throw random colours on a piece of paper, and people will call it art. Throw random musical notes on a piano, and people will call it crap.

246. They are called light-years because you can't measure anything in the dark.

258. I would be proud to end my life on earth without ending it myself.

263. A bunker is not seen, yet it is very imposing when facing a catastrophe.

102. Artificial intelligence is a fraction of human capacity that can die once the energy source is cut off.

117. The higher you go, the more transparent people's ambition becomes.

120. If I look back occasionally, I want to check that the tail is still there.

171. The wind - you don't know where it's coming from or where it's going to, and yet it can be rather beneficial when planned in silence.

177. A woman does not have to arrange too much to be beautiful, but a man has to make big arrangements to attract beauty.

190. Why would I let a blind man tell me what the light looks like, and why would I let a deaf man criticise the sound of my words?

198. We have become a world where political analysis is done on musical notes and those on the verge of hepatitis release prescriptions.

200. A nuclear bomb will not destroy only buildings and people, but people only. Buildings are the dreams of people who have come true through work.

203. A smile on the face cannot wipe the tears secretly gathered.

207. I am a simple man due to its well-managed complexity.

208. If I am correcting something I have written, it is because I want the work that I will hand over at the end to be placed near perfection.

209. When children talk like adults, the world is on the verge of bankruptcy.

214. Poverty dances in the streets, wealth crumbles in luxury hotels, and freedom cries in open prisons. A real-world for no one to give.

215. Do not vomit the normal as if it was something toxic; later, you will not be able to chew it as something delicious.

221. The only thing that you can do once you raise a puppy that bites you after you feed it, is to step aside as soon as it has grown.

225. If you're not taking notes of the past, don't expect to know how to act now to change something in the future.

235. The weather in England is very changeable today (2022), more exactly like people.

265. Why did no one succeed in taking the lion cub next to his mother to teach him how to live in the jungle? Because once it's taken, it becomes a circus animal.

267. If you could film the camera, I would show what I have in my pockets. At the moment, I'm capturing the attention of others.

271. If there is any free time, I would use it to weed with the hoe of knowledge the weeds of the intelligence of the world.

272. I am not a man for rapid development but rather for an easy rise in society by giving each piece of information received the time necessary to increase understanding and to have it implemented at the right time.

279. When you water a tree, even the smallest ones have the shade and protection they need to grow. When you water only the small ones, the tree dries out.

280. The lower blanket and the upper blanket of society are separated; both can create comfort if you know which to use and when.

282. Why do we all want to know what the future holds for us when we know so little about the treasures of the past that were the tool to create the present?

286. A beaten lion does not want to listen to a barking dog because he is licking his wounds and does not mind having the prey shared. However, if the dog does not stop barking, it can easily become silent and part of the lion's food.

287. Lend me your ears so I can talk.

289. When a slave to society becomes rich, all he wants is to buy freedom, and when he gets it, he ends up being locked in the desert of knowledge.

292. The information can become an addiction for some; that's how the legal dealers appeared. Some are selling it for a living, I will do it for fun.

293. Anyone who knows how to use a pen can write history.

312. To be able to sell my work to me, you have to put me in the difficulty of needing that thing.

318. A woman should not be beautiful and smart but rather healthy and wise.

327. Even if I am a professional driver, I cannot be responsible for the car's direction if I'm not in the driver's seat.

329. Unfortunately, education in some countries is so sought after that if you say something stupid with intonation, it is received as something intelligent and vital. It's like showing a poor bait of polenta, and the fish jumps like crazy in the bucket.

335. Possessing a name absent of wealth is like singing a song without sound.

337. Standing against modern technology is like trying to catch the power of the wind with your bare hands.

344. The only time when a woman raises or shortens her skirt is when she wants to walk through mud and dirt.

352. The only way to burn the well-dressed lies is to confront them with the naked truth.

366. Up to your 30s, you need support; from your 30s to your 50s, you work to become support; after your 50s, you are a support. Stop messing them around.

370. When you get dirty, you need a proper man to clean it up.

373. If there is someone in the room who talks and someone who thinks and wrote the speech, who takes the bullet if there is an assassination?

381. I saw the back of the world and realised it is naked in all pride.

383. People are not born stupid; people become stupid over time, because they don't use their brains.

387. Only a piece of trash struggles to hold on to a well-polished slipper.

416. A nuclear weapon, even if not used, defuses powers through fear of its existence.

418. To repair a broken vessel, it is necessary to spill the content into another vessel for a while. The more the vessel is kept with content while broken, the more its repair is delayed and may be beyond repair. Trying to save the contents may cause the loss of the vessel.

442. If my body identifies certain genders, why would that be wrong? If someone thinks that this is wrong, the question should not be addressed to the invention but to the inventor.

467. The difference between the words given by the one who did not take action and the one who took action about the one who takes action is enormous. The criticism of the inexperienced is close to condemnation, while that of the experienced is gracious. Be gracious!

472. Time is scary because, despite human attempts, it has not been stopped by any, has seen a lot, and is persistent in its precision.

Chapter 6: Humour

I. The thought of a man who became so rich as to turn his money with the shovel: *"I have used the shovel to get rich and retire. Now I use the shovel to turn money; why was I so impatient to get rich?"*

II. *"What you see now is an exotic presentation. I'm coming from the kitchen. Many ingredients have been taken off the floor or reused. Enjoy watching."*

III. When asked his age, a man answered: *"I have them all; from birth till now, I've jumped no year."*

IV. When people say: *"You sound like an idiot"*.
What they actually want to say is: *"You didn't understand what I have tried to tell you because I cannot explain in words what I want to say."*
This is what makes them clever.

V. When people ask me how old I am, I reply: *"I do not know my exact age, but on the earth, I've got the age count from 1993."*

VI. Only one out of approximately 300 million spermatozoa helps the egg to be fertilised, and yet God says that he knows your name before you were born, from the foundation of the world, and not a single hair falls without His knowledge. *"How could some explosion create the world we live in so perfect for life, and how could some explosion create a self-regenerating mechanism with the ability to create?"*

VII.   Someone asked me once: *"You have a nice car, sir, what do you do for a living?"*;
I replied: *"I'm a construction manager"*;
Then he added: *"Does the university help?"*;
I said: *"Of course not, but what I have learned there, yes."*

VIII.   I asked myself: *"Why are people placed with their hands on their chests when they die? If they were placed with their hands in their pockets, they wouldn't have been noticed by the living that they are leaving this world empty-handed. "*

IX.   Talking to someone likewise: *"When God felt empty, he created man; man, who was, after the likeness of God, empty. When God saw that man was empty, He created woman; a woman who was taken from man, after the likeness of God, empty. When God saw that the woman was empty, he told the man to enter to her, and the woman became pregnant and gave birth to a child."*
Moral: Emptiness is the root of creation.